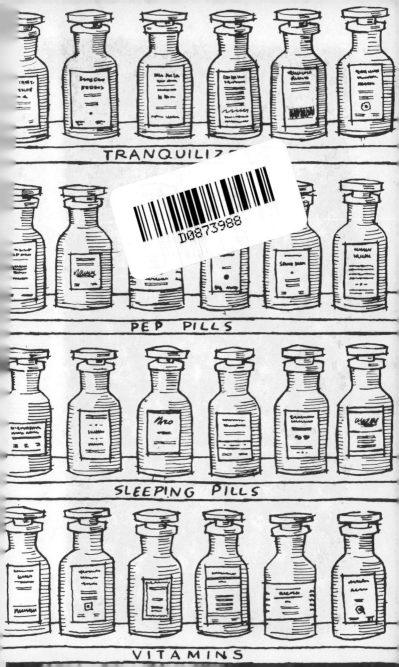

The Second Neurotic's Notebook

by Mignon McLaughlin

THE NEUROTIC'S NOTEBOOK

The SECOND NEUROTIC'S Notebook

MIGNON McLAUGHLIN

THE BOBBS-MERRILL COMPANY, INC.

A SUBSIDIARY OF HOWARD W. SAMS & CO., INC.

PUBLISHERS   INDIANAPOLIS   NEW YORK   KANSAS CITY

Parts of this book, in slightly altered form, have appeared in *The Atlantic Monthly, Glamour,* and *The Reader's Digest;* also in many newspaper and magazine columns; and even, without permission, in Chinese fortune cookies.

Contents

Dedicated, lovingly,
to my sons Thomas and James

The Second Neurotic's Notebook

1 Love and Marriage

Women are right about love: it's better than housework any day.

When love goes wrong, a man wants to walk out, a woman to stay and cry.

Men marry sexy little girls for some *other* quality, as they never tire of telling you.

We all become great explorers during our first few days in a new city, or a new love affair.

If your husband expects you to laugh, do so; if he expects you to cry, don't; if you don't know what he expects, what are you doing married?

I

Every wife who doesn't much love her husband considers it his fault.

Love is to man an embarrassment, even the word; it is to women an excuse for existence, especially the word.

A woman's convinced that love will last, a man that it won't; and you know which is more often surprised.

Lovers' quarrels end in kisses, each a little less innocent than the one before.

The more serious your love affair, the more people will find it ridiculous.

Hateful pretty women always get married, and so do an amazing number of hateful homely ones.

No sensible woman ever *asks* her husband whether or not to color her hair.

2

Naturally, the neurotic wants you to love him twice as much, for he's going to cut it in half anyway.

If you see right through him, it's because you do not want him.

Two who embark on a love affair, both knowing it's not likely to last, deserve the worst they get—which is apt to be pretty bad.

If you habitually quarrel with the one you love, you might as well learn to enjoy it.

Marriage represents the intervention of the state in a love affair which probably wasn't going too well anyway.

When a husband and wife agree all the time, he's henpecked.

People often say they love each other when they really don't, but it's strange how often just saying it makes it come true.

Many quarrels are murmuringly resolved in bed. And many silently start there.

A love that lasts for twenty years may be better than love, but it isn't love.

Affairs are just as disillusioning as marriage, and much less restful.

If you can't resolve a quarrel gracefully, don't get married.

When two neurotics marry, there is no one to listen.

Love requires a willingness to die; marriage, a willingness to live.

4

f you keep falling in and out of love with others, you grow shallow. If they keep falling in and out of love with you, you grow brutalized.

When a man's wife and his mistress get cozy together, it's time for both of them —no, for all three of them—to move on.

Shrew: a woman who doesn't know her own strength till she finds her husband's weakness.

When a man stops being in love with you, it's no consolation to remind yourself that you may not have been in love with him in the first place.

A woman asks little of love: only that she be able to feel like a heroine.

Marriage is the refuge of the very lonely, and the very self-sufficient.

5

Long engagements make everyone nervous, and are therefore a good rehearsal for marriage.

The difference, in love, between normal people and neurotic ones: the neurotic sees more clearly the end of love coming, but is just as powerless to stop it.

Women completely plot the course of every love affair, and are completely wrong.

A woman's mink coat represents the sacrifice of a lot of little animals, including her husband.

Never cross-question your husband about what kept him so late; he might discover how easy it is to lie.

You will never again be so self-centered as in the midst of a selfless love affair.

6

A good marriage winds up as a meeting of minds, which had better be pretty good to start with.

Love is fact for women, fiction for men.

A first-rate marriage is like a first-rate hotel: expensive, but worth it.

In the arithmetic of love, one plus one equals everything, and two minus one equals nothing.

A woman needs at least one man on whom to test her sense of power; he's the wrong man to marry, though.

You can't put too much liking into loving. (Whichever meaning you give this one, you're right.)

Love fills a man's eyes with smiles, a woman's with tears.

Love is often gentle, desire always a rage.

How it rejoices a middle-aged woman when her husband criticizes a pretty girl!

Women insist upon marriage and then hate it; men are dragged there and then love it.

Reminder to clever wives: it's better to be kind than witty, and practically impossible to be both.

All real twosomes are the only one in the world.

Trust is to love as icing to cake: not strictly necessary, but it sure sweetens the taste.

A man will desert the wife he loves more often than the type he loves.

8

There's no such thing as an innocent flirtation—only one which doesn't quite make it.

If you're really in love, you'll keep seeing him, even in crowds he's not in.

Of the few happy marriages a neurotic sees around him, most seem unsuitable.

You might as well withdraw love as threaten to withdraw it; to one who loves you, these are equal catastrophes.

Advice to women who remarry: never spell out to your second husband how much you loved, or hated, your first.

If marriage is your object, you'd better start by loving your subject.

We can all do without love, but not much.

9

Old maids are sooner satisfied than wives.

Neurotics marry and tell themselves that things will change. It's like writing poetry on a typewriter: possible, but just barely.

At the beginning of a love affair, not even the neurotic is neurotic.

"What's for dinner?" is the only question many husbands ask their wives, and the only one to which they care about the answer.

There are three iron links in the neurotic's chain: unloving, unlovable, unloved.

No wife can forgive her husband for saying angry things to her and then placidly going to sleep.

A woman with a good husband, and sons, will flirt till the day she dies.

To the neurotic, each love affair seems like a curtain going up for the first time, each quarrel like a curtain going down forever.

A successful marriage requires falling in love many times, always with the same person.

A man will overlook much in his wife, if she just doesn't keep him waiting.

With the neurotic, it's never too late for someone to love him—only too late to do him any good.

A husband only worries about a particular Other Man; a wife distrusts her whole species.

Love unlocks doors and opens windows that weren't even there before.

All love is probationary, a fact which frightens women and exhilarates men.

Some marriages break up, and some do not, and in our world you can usually explain the former better than the latter.

Separate rooms are a luxury no happily married couple can afford.

2 Home and Children

It's easy enough to get along with a loved and loving child—at least till you try to get him to do something.

What were you deprived of in childhood? You have it now and why aren't you happy?

The young are often full of revolt, and they're often pretty revolting about it.

There's one desirable place to be long-winded: in letters back home.

One woman will brag about her children, while another complains about hers; they could probably swap children without swapping tunes.

The way to find out about daughters: have sons.

If your child doesn't think you're wonderful, you certainly aren't.

There is no way to repay a mother's love, or lack of it.

That home is happy where the refrigerator cleans itself.

There's an awful lot of blood around that water is thicker than.

No matter how many Christmas presents you give your child, there's always that terrible moment when he's opened the very last one. That's when he expects you to say, "Oh yes, I almost forgot," and take him out and show him the pony.

Suburb: a place that isn't city, isn't country, and isn't tolerable.

In adolescence, our children's complexions erupt, and so do their feelings. Our inadequate prescription for both: frequent cold showers.

Likely as not, the child you can do the least with will do the most to make you proud.

Ma-ma does everything for the baby, who responds by saying Da-da first.

Best neurotic way to show your children you regard them as grownups: quarrel fiercely with them.

I hope that when the time comes, I'll be a good mother-in-law. I have only one qualification for it: I always love the girls who love my sons.

Our children seem to have wonderful taste, or none—depending, of course, on whether or not they agree with us.

Watching *their* little girl in a Christmas pageant, most parents feel as if they'd just discovered Garbo.

Never let your children be greater snobs than you are.

A woman who didn't love her mother will never quite believe that her children love *her*.

Your children vividly remember every unkind thing you ever did to them, plus a few you really didn't.

Setting up headquarters for your teen-aged children and their friends? Make it Liberty Hall, a mile or so this side of Licenseville.

We don't mind our children having different virtues from ours, but it seems disloyal of them to have different faults.

A happy child is a great testimonial to his parents, but only if they think he did it all himself.

A loving mother has to find *some* way of expressing it, so she nags at you to eat.

A parent who has never apologized to his children is a monster. If he's *always* apologizing, his children are monsters.

A marriage without children is like a Chinese dinner without rice: the flavor may be there, but not the substance.

Families who hate each other seem almost glued together; a happy home is such a free place that there is seldom anyone in it.

I used to worry that I'd have fat chil
dren who'd glare at me and say "Oh
Mother!" Instead, I have thin children
who glare at me and say "Oh, *Mother!*"

The little of my childhood that I can remember is the part I still play out today.

Always plan on a traditional family
Christmas dinner, and a traditional family fight afterward.

For the neurotic—anywhere he hangs
himself is home.

Children are the noisiest creatures on
earth, but they never forgive a mother
who screams at them.

If your children spend most of their time
in other people's houses, you're lucky; if
they all congregate at your house, you're
blessed.

18

The ideal home: big enough for you to hear the children, but not very well.

Daddy asks his daughter "Whose little girl are you?", and Mommy has her first twinge of jealousy.

Nobody has a happy childhood, said a young man who was the happiest child I ever knew.

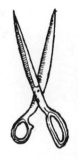

Your children tell you casually years later what it would have killed you with worry to know at the time.

3 Men and Women

Men are convinced that women have it easy, but they haven't convinced many women.

Men gossip less than women, but mean it.

There's no one so ruthless as a timid woman striking back.

The way to a man's heart is through his stomach, especially if you tell him how flat it is.

Trust a woman, and not a man, in casual moments; a man, and not a woman, in crucial ones. For that's when each tends to tell the truth.

Shopping brings out gluttony in a woman, impatience in a man.

Ask a woman why she's so happy, and she'll immediately wonder if she is.

The woman just ahead of you at the supermarket checkout has all the delectable groceries you didn't even know they carried.

She was a real pet: both dogged and catty.

Women let you know how awful they really feel, and how bravely they're concealing it.

Women who feel naked without their lipstick are well over thirty.

No one really listens to anyone else, and if you try it for a while you'll see why.

A man will do anything to win a certain woman; afterwards, he thinks he must have been crazy.

Good-looking girls break hearts, and goodhearted girls mend them.

No woman wants to see herself too clearly.

Many beautiful women have been made happy by their own beauty, but no intelligent woman has ever been made happy by her own intelligence.

Men who wear glasses forever make passes.

Many a quarrel has been deferred by a woman's tears—but not for long.

Women are afraid of mice and of murder, and of very little in between.

Man: a creature who runs out of money even faster than he runs out of love.

When a man falls in love, he wants to go to bed. When a woman falls in love, she wants to talk about it.

"If I've told you once, I've told you a thousand times." That's every woman's autobiography.

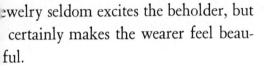

Jewelry seldom excites the beholder, but it certainly makes the wearer feel beautiful.

The average woman's a success if she pleases one man; the great beauty's a failure if one man gets away.

To have the best of both worlds, women should spend their days in the company of women, their nights in the company of men.

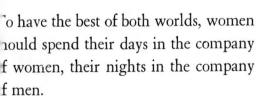

Most women, like small children, enjoy saying no; and most men, like idiots take them seriously.

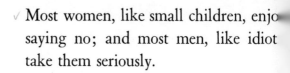

Nothing brings out the gallantry in man like his daughter's pretty friends.

The meekest woman is merely a Becky Sharp whose nerve has failed her.

Men want a woman both sexy and lady like, women want a man at once rough and tender. Isn't it wonderful when both imagine themselves satisfied?

A woman will keep on dating men she abhors, hoping they'll introduce her to men she adores.

Women are invariably at their most beautiful when with men they care nothing about.

t needs only an attractive man to sepa-
ate the women from the girls.

know that women throng to every
ports event, but you'll never convince
ne that any of them really enjoy it.

'ew women care what a man looks like,
nd a good thing too.

3y the time women are kind to each
ther, they're no longer rivals.

No matter what she looks like, every
woman secretly considers herself rather
eductive.

t's in the nature of some women to wait
or the man who wants them, of others
o go after the man they want; it's im-
oortant for every woman to decide
which type she is.

Women are appalled by men's reckless-
ness; men are reassured by women's lack
of it.

A woman will do anything to keep a
pretty figure, but hardly anything to get
one.

Men really prefer reasonably attractive
women; they go after the sensational
ones to impress other men.

A woman will wear her heart on her
sleeve, if she thinks it goes with her
dress.

A woman on a diet soon feels like
Joan of Arc.

If a woman can get a man to talk to her
about himself, she can get him to pro-
pose. Especially if he's unmarried at
the time.

t's wonderful to watch a pretty woman with character grow beautiful.

Women want to be treated as women all of the time, and as ladies half of the time.

All women are basically in competition with each other for a handful of eligible men.

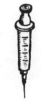

Sarcasm, like haemophilia, is transmitted by the females of the family.

Women dress to please themselves, or their husbands, or their women friends. Any wardrobe that really satisfies one of these groups will enrage the other two.

With men, as with women, the main struggle is between vanity and comfort; but with men, comfort often wins.

Women's chatter bores men, but no half so much as it bores women.

A woman alone in Venice is like a man two years out of work.

Women simultaneously adore and suspect any bachelor over thirty.

Men are more honest than women, but you need a microscope to discover it.

There are three kinds of women: those who enjoy losing to a man, those who enjoy losing to a woman, and those who just enjoy losing.

Women are never landlocked: they're always mere minutes away from the briny deep of tears.

Men enjoy being thought of as hunters, but are generally too lazy to hunt.

Women, on the other hand, love to hunt, but would rather nobody knew it.

Men who don't like girls with brains don't like girls.

Women talk and talk, but men hear only the self-incriminating things.

The sole demand on a beautiful girl is to say "Thank you" nicely when people say "You're beautiful."

With two people who can really talk to each other, sex is no more than a marvelous bonus. And vice versa.

Baseball is really for everybody: women neither throw nor catch as well as men, but they cross home plate more often.

Fortunately, not everyone who could kill you does.

Women claim to be intuitive, but they're always stunned when men stop loving them.

Every man is unique whose wife makes him feel so.

In every roué, there's a bit of Peter Pan—impervious, though, to the Wendy in a woman.

√Hate leaves ugly scars, love leaves beautiful ones.

√Some women love only what they can hold in their arms; others, only what they can't.

Ask a woman how she feels, and she tells you. Ask a lady, and she says, "Fine, thank you."

f you must reread old love letters, better
ick a room without mirrors.

Most men are prepared to fight if they
have to, but most women are not prepared to let them.

4 Health, Happiness, and Self-Esteem

Nobody knows the trouble we've seen— but we keep trying to tell them.

Neurotics dream of a good life, or a great suicide note.

Forget about calories—*everything* makes thin people thinner, and fat people fatter.

Ours is not the only story, just the most interesting one.

The first night of your stay in a hospital, you're given a heavenly backrub by an angel you never set eyes on again.

The neurotic feels as though trapped in a gas-filled room where at any moment someone, probably himself, will strike a match.

Always live up to your standards—by lowering them, if necessary.

They threaten me with lung cancer, and still I smoke and smoke. If they'd only threaten me with hard work, I might stop.

Don't be yourself—be someone a little nicer.

Neurotics deal with anxiety by clinging to half a rope halfway down a well.

The only patience the neurotic knows is that to be found in a bottle of sleeping pills.

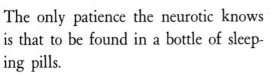

33

Most of us are pretty good at postponing our nervous breakdowns till we can afford them.

For the happiest life, rigorously plan your days, leave your nights open to chance.

As every woman knows, laugh and the world laughs with you; cry and some man will comfort you.

Offices are full of people who are only alive from Monday to Friday.

I know it's happened, but I'm damned if I know how: the survival of innocent people in Germany, 1940, and in Mississippi, 1965.

Our protestations don't often fool others, but they still serve a purpose: they fool *us*.

34

Go on a diet, quit smoking, give up alcohol—but not all at once.

If you are neurotic and wish to hide it, go easy on coffee, pills, cigarettes, and alcohol—and keep your mouth shut.

A cynic is one who believes it matters not whether you win, *nor* how you play the game.

People will disapprove of you if you're unhappy, or if you're happy in The Wrong Way.

It wasn't just with Mark Twain: the reports of *all* deaths are greatly exaggerated.

Neurotics always feel as though they were going way up or way down, which is odd in people going sideways.

I can't figure out why, but hangovers always make me terribly courteous.

The neurotic usually obeys his own Golden Rule: Hate thy neighbor as thy-self.

Grasp your opportunities, no matter how poor your health; *nothing* is worse for your health than boredom.

You can't truthfully explain your smallest action without fully revealing your character.

There's nothing wrong with most men's egos that the kowtowing of a head-waiter can't cure.

We're all lovable. At least in our own eyes. At least if you catch us at the right moment.

If you hate your lot but wouldn't trade it, it's not your lot you hate.

A sense of humor is a major defense against minor troubles.

A small cut on one of my fingertips keeps reopening, and it's a brand-new thrill: seeing your own blood on the typewriter keys.

Without sex, alcohol, sleeping pills, you are always with yourself.

Nothing so rousingly raises your spirits as emerging from a gloomy movie into a sunny afternoon.

Neurotics are always looking for something new to overdo.

Charm makes everyone feel wonderful except, often, its possessor.

People who make the best of a bad bargain automatically have the beginnings of a good one.

A hypochondriac is one who has a pill for everything except what ails him.

Speak up when it's time to, whether it's your turn or not.

If you must be sick, do it interestingly: faint or something.

Character is what emerges from all the little things you were too busy to do yesterday, but did anyway.

Other people's truth may comfort us, but only our own persuades us.

Failure can get to be a rather comfortable old friend.

I've just posed for a portrait, and it's an experience I recommend: the one time in your life when you can do absolutely nothing, and feel virtuous about it.

Neurotic: someone who can go from the bottom to the top, and back again, without ever once touching the middle.

Love, at best, is joy; work, though, can be ecstasy.

The two things that make office life endurable: coffee breaks, and falling in love.

Halfway through exciting work is halfway to heaven.

Convinced that you're not ungrateful to others, but they are to you? Congratulations; you're a true neurotic.

Acedia is not in every dictionary; just in every heart.

 Tough and funny and a little bit kind: that is as near to perfection as a human being can be.

Being neurotic is like shooting fish in a barrel, and missing them.

 Neurotics are sure that no one understands them, and they wouldn't have it any other way.

It's terrifying to see someone inside of whom a vital spring seems to have broken. It's particularly terrifying to see him in your mirror.

 There's no such thing as a humdrum life; to the person living it, it's all peaks and abysses.

Few individuals can survive repeated cycles of misfortune, but whole races do it all the time.

Of course no one is so sensitive as you, but try to remember they *think* they are.

If you find yourself a bit ridiculous, you can scarcely expect to be able to take anyone else very seriously.

Hammock reading is egghead stuff to a hammock reader.

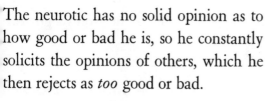

The neurotic has no solid opinion as to how good or bad he is, so he constantly solicits the opinions of others, which he then rejects as *too* good or bad.

Some people never get hooked on anything; but among those who do, it's never just one thing.

When we say "If I don't do it, someone else will," we mean, of course, some other son of a bitch.

Never turn down the chance of an adventure, unless such chances are coming thick and fast, and maybe not even then.

The only courage that matters is the kind that gets you from one moment to the next.

Neurotics are anxiety prone, accident prone, and often just prone.

If you've got the talent, you've got the energy.

The next voice you hear will undoubtedly be your own.

5 The General Orneriness of Things

Things are never so bad that they can't get worse. But they're sometimes so bad they can't get better.

Good food, good sex, good digestion, good sleep: to these basic animal pleasures, man has added nothing but the good cigarette.

If I knew what I was so anxious about, I wouldn't be so anxious.

The neurotic desperately galvanizes his energy, and produces an aftercast: i.e., "a throw of dice after the game is ended; hence, anything done too late."

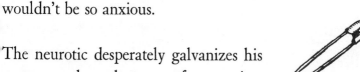

There is no way to say "I love you" in English.

Your best work always seems to have been done by someone else.

If they dare to cross-examine you, you're ruined; the really strong, no one dares to cross-examine.

A little suffering exalts us, a little success encourages us, a little pleasure comforts us. The trouble is, it never remains a little.

The way the neurotic sees it: bars on his door mean that he's locked in; bars on your door mean that he's locked out.

Love gives no warning and no quarter; it is sneaky and cruel; if we weren't so lonely, we'd never put up with it.

Most of us become parents long before we have stopped being children.

We vaguely know the rules, and the system of scoring, but for God's sake why don't they tell us how long the game is?

Youth is not enough. And love is not enough. And success is not enough. And, if we could achieve it, enough would not be enough.

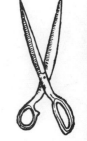

If you are brave too often, people will come to expect it of you.

Life is a mixed blessing, which we vainly try to unmix.

You can trust a sentimental person, every time, to be merciless.

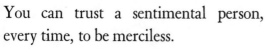

Every martyr comes with a built-in bully.

A generous woman, a man with empathy, a cabdriver who keeps his mouth shut: these almost do not exist.

The head never rules the heart, but just becomes its partner in crime.

"Let your conscience be your guide" is a silly thing to say to a good man, or a bad one.

Fields can lie fallow, but we can't; we have less time.

Strong cruel women generally marry weak cruel men.

Sisyphus is the only one for whom it was a myth.

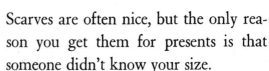

Scarves are often nice, but the only reason you get them for presents is that someone didn't know your size.

The best people seldom give you the best advice.

The trouble with ingenues: by the time a pretty young girl learns anything about acting, she's no longer a pretty young girl.

With each passing year, one has less to say, and knows better how to say it.

You know how you hate being interrupted, so why are you always doing it to me?

I know a man who married a woman he didn't love, because he thought that everyone else did. They still do, and he still doesn't.

Sensible reason to cheat at solitaire: you want *something* to come out right, just *once*.

When you're about to issue that well-deserved ultimatum, just stop for a moment and remember the last time.

The only language some people understand is the one Berlitz doesn't teach.

There have been cases of couples getting married who first met on a blind date—but your chances of winning the Irish Sweepstakes are slightly better.

Live and let live: now there's a pair of impossible commands!

Neurotics chase after people and jobs they don't really want, just to prove that they're like everybody else—which is the *last* thing they really want.

We always prefer war on our own terms to peace on someone else's.

The time we can often do something wonderful is when we are supposed to be doing something else.

When you're nervous it makes you cranky, and when you're cranky it makes people hostile, and when people are hostile it makes you nervous.

When anyone gets the fate he deserves, it's quite coincidental.

This morning, our twenty-year-old son enlisted in the Naval Air Reserve. You wait and wait for something to happen; then that's the sort of thing that happens.

The only totally benign inventions of our times: Kleenex, and the electric percolator.

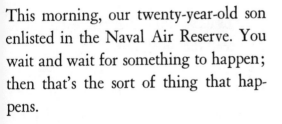

We semaphore from ship to ship, but they're sinking, too.

People find it hard to be both comic and serious, though life manages it easily enough.

Few men have ever been able to resist doing the things that bring out the shrew in a woman.

People are like birds: on the wing, all beautiful; up close, all beady little eyes.

Most of us would rather risk catastrophe than read the directions.

There are different clothes in everyone's closet, but always the same old skeletons.

Most of us can easily do two things at once; what's all but impossible is to do one thing at once.

Today's wondrous household appliances
have made things much easier, but only
for the *good* housekeepers.

The time to begin most things is ten
years ago.

6 Friends and Enemies

Anywhere you go liking everyone, everyone will be likable.

The neurotic keeps minute track of his enemies; it is only his friends he is careless about.

If people find your silences interesting, don't disillusion them.

No matter how many times you change jobs or mates or neighborhoods, there's always *someone* in your life you can't get along with.

When you're with people you have nothing to say to, you're liable to say almost anything.

The neurotic never has friends: just enemies and potential enemies.

It takes charm to win over sulky people
—charm and a willingness to waste
your time.

Before you go, hope they remember you;
before you return, hope they've forgotten.

Once over lightly works better for eggs
than for people.

Few of us could bear to have ourselves
for neighbors.

Anybody can sit and talk all night, but
it takes iron discipline to listen for fifteen
minutes.

Nothing so blights a party as a hostess
with plans for making it jolly.

Don't tell the neurotic your name or address or anything else irrelevant; all he wants to know is whether you're for him or against him.

The neurotic always wishes people would let him alone—until they do.

If no one will meet your eye, stop trying to tell your story.

There are people who hide their love from you, and people who hide their hate, and you'll be wise to stay away from both.

Coming across an old friend you haven't seen for years is like finding a forgotten suit in the back of the closet: you're glad to see it, but you soon discover it doesn't fit any more.

Bribes and punishments are equally unavailing against the real don't-cares.

When humorless people laugh loudest and longest, it's a signal to the rest of us that they've had enough of our wit.

Every group has its favorite clown, and it's Rule One that he be unhappy.

Surrounded by people who love life, you love it too; surrounded by people who don't, you don't.

It's easier to part with a friend than an opinion.

To talk easily with people, you must firmly believe that either you or they are interesting. And even then it's not easy.

If a man likes his wife's best friend at all, he likes her too much.

People credit you with only half of what you have done—but blame you for only half, too.

Neurotics have plenty of non-neurotic friends, but not for long.

We never mind snobs who like *us*.

People who like you at your worst aren't really suitable for you at your best.

Those who are brutally honest are seldom so with themselves.

On converting an enemy into a friend, rejoice—but don't relax.

We're seldom drawn to a character we admire; only to a personality we like.

Duty seldom prompts us to tell people flattering things.

56

I'd like to be liked by everybody, because when people like me I usually like them, and I'd like to like everybody.

A friend: one who pretends he's as interested in your welfare as in his own.

An enemy: one who has his own best welfare at heart, not yours.

An acquaintance: somebody you nod to if he nods first.

A bore: one who knows as well as you do what he is going to say next.

Friendships don't last long when they're used as wailing walls.

The neurotic lies awake at night, composing letters to those he hates. He seldom thinks of dropping a line to those he loves.

57

Villains: people who do the same things that we do, but we have the right reasons.

Resuming a long-interrupted friendship makes you feel half your age, and double it.

Neurotics would change places with anyone—except the people they know.

Never ask a hypochondriac how he is, nor a bore what he's been doing.

Every now and then you run across radiantly attractive people, and you're delighted to find they adore you, till you realize that they adore just about everybody—and that's what's made them radiantly attractive.

Heat blisters skin, and paint, and friendship.

58

If you started the rumor and it comes **b**ack to you substantially unchanged, **y**ou've got some mighty dull neighbors.

There are some people we just plain **d**on't like the looks of, and they all nestle **c**lose to us on the beach..

7 Politics, Arts, Professions

My doctor is nice; every time I see him I'm ashamed of what I think of doctors in general.

Politics makes strange bedfellows, but so do beds.

A door-to-door salesman must have a personality as appealing as a movie star's, and for a small fraction of the pay.

The chief function of an executive is to keep those who really do the work from doing it in peace.

The Liberal: conservatives see him as a dupe; radicals see him as a coward; even in his own eyes, he's no great bargain.

A moderate is one who has rejected extremes, at least for the moment.

A subversive: one who doesn't like Walt Disney *or* Coca-Cola.

Neurotics make poor patriots; if you're ashamed of something as big as yourself, it's hard to be proud of something as small as your country.

A gifted teacher is as rare as a gifted doctor, and makes far less money.

If you really can't bear to do shabby things, forget about being an executive.

A recent survey was said to prove that the people we Americans most admire are our politicians and doctors. I don't believe it. They're simply the people we're most afraid of. And with the most reason.

In the hardware business, as in the theatre, the show must go on; it's just that actors make a bigger fuss about it.

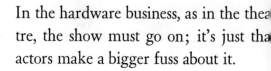

In medicine, no practitioner likes to charge another with malpractice. Among artists, it's the favorite pastime.

There's no art form so sophisticated that the experts can't be fooled by the work of a clever child.

Conservatives worry about government extravagance, liberals about government heartlessness. Conservatives have the advantage: it's much easier to identify extravagance.

Peace and Prosperity make nice campaign slogans. And who knows? They might even work some day, on some other planet.

When a nation has been defeated and loses its pride, a leader always springs up who restores it, in psychopathic doses.

Few novels or plays could exist without at least one troublemaker in the group, and perhaps life couldn't either.

I hate to think of all the young doctors this minute dreaming of discovering a brand-new disease, so it can be named for them.

The greatest works of art and the vilest murders are motivated alike: to do one thing once that only you in all the world can do.

There's only one person who needs a glass of water oftener than a small child tucked in for the night, and that's a writer sitting down to write.

In Utopia, people will study art, an artists will study life.

Watch yourself on your first job: it's perfect forecast of all jobs to come.

A doctor recently described to me "benign positional vertigo": it means you get dizzy in certain positions, but you can get over it without necessarily changing the position. Change "vertigo" to "anxiety," and you've summed up the neurotic's plight.

When a chef, a chemist, a tree surgeon talks about his work, we can all listen and learn; let an artist do it, though, and it just sounds pretentious.

Creative people usually head for the big cities: more than the theatres, museums or libraries, they need each other.

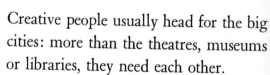

Women vie with men for a lot of jobs that neither men nor women want.

To write the best possible play, start off with the best possible exposition scene, then go ahead and finish the play, then go back and lop off the exposition scene.

Of all second-class citizens, neurotics are the only ones who are so by choice.

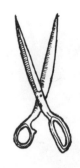

Creative work is one of life's greatest pleasures, and the only one we will gladly interrupt.

Talent is one muscle no one has ever overexercised.

It's my theory that Murray Kempton and William Buckley are merely alternate pen names of the same exasperating man.

Nowhere but in the arts can talent, ex perience, dedication, and years of har work lead to a steady decline in qualit

Has there ever been a time when it wa not respectable to be conservative?

When threatened, the first thing a d mocracy gives up is democracy.

The Best People sometimes join a ba movement early, but they seldom join good movement till almost too late.

There's no subject that a skillful write can't make Americans laugh at, or cr at—except maybe Canada.

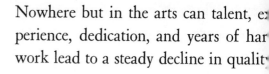

The artist and the housewife have this i common: though both can arbitraril call it quits when they want to, neithe can ever with certainty say: There i nothing more to be done.

took man thousands of years to put
words down on paper, and his lawyers
ill wish he wouldn't.

admire J. D. Salinger, but I think it's
me he left the Glass Menagerie to
ennessee Williams.

he last selfless doctor I can remember
as Jean Hersholt.

8 God and the Devil

I dare to drink the water when there i reason to doubt, yet cannot make th same concession to God.

Minor vices lead to major ones, bu minor virtues stay put.

Neurotics are afraid to pray: God migh be listening.

Many cleaners now give same-day serv ice, which is more than most religion. can promise you.

Purgatory must be like that momen when you first wake, just before you remember that you love and are loved

My religious position: I think that God could do a lot better, and I'm willing to give Him the chance.

Come Judgment Day, two groups alone will be saved: the cheerful, and the devout.

God doesn't measure His bounty, but oh how *we* do!

I half-believe in reincarnation, and I'd like to come back as an otter; so far as I know, it's impossible to be a bad otter.

Never is a long, long word, but it's less frustrating than "God knows when."

Anti-Semitism will still be the Number One problem among Jews long after it has disappeared from the rest of the world.

A movement takes on strength when people are willing to die for it, but it doesn't necessarily take on virtue.

I know someone who is both evil and boring, which is surely a case of the devil doing God's work for Him.

If you lie all the time, you'll soon be the only one fooled by it.

I can't believe that God minds the disbelief of the young.

Most of our diversions do not so much delay death as accustom us to it.

There are, we used to be told, no atheists in foxholes. (I'm not even sure there are any foxholes any more.) And there are, apparently, no atheists in the Ku Klux Klan. God sometimes moves in mysterious ways, His lip service to exact.

70

The neurotic believes that life has meaning, but that *his* life hasn't.

The devil finds plenty of mischief for loving hands to do.

If you truly believe in God, and the immortality of the soul, why do you get so mad when a malefactor goes unpunished?

I've been hiding from God, and I'm appalled to find how easy it is.

Basis for a workable religion: when you have nothing better to do, do something for someone else.

The timid shall love and comfort the timid, and remain timid.

The young do not need God, and the old cannot find Him.

The Bible leads us to some strange conclusions: for instance, that Paradise is for lunatics—since they, like Adam and Eve, have no knowledge of good or evil.

Most sermons sound to me like commercials—but I can't make out whether God is the Sponsor or the Product.

"Your money, or your life." We know what to do when a burglar makes this demand of us, but not when God does.

Puritans will never believe it, but life is full of disagreeable things that aren't even good for you.

Don't look for God where He is needed most; if you didn't bring Him there, He isn't there.

The neurotic's constant prayer: that nothing *worse* will happen.

I know a young man who doesn't believe in God, but does believe in the devil; it's my hunch that God finds this acceptable.

If you take the high road and I take the low road, naturally I'll get there before you.

There's something in every atheist, itching to believe, and something in every believer, itching to doubt.

I often pray, though I'm not really sure Anyone's listening; and I phrase it carefully, just in case He's literary.

9 Getting and Spending

Philosophy teaches a man that he can't take it with him; taxes teach him he can't leave it behind either.

Money equalizes all people who were equal to begin with.

What to do with a windfall: spend a little, save a little, gamble a little, pay some bills with what's left.

Furniture dealer: one who will offer to buy your best Edwardian chest for the price you had hoped to get for the kitchen table.

A rich suicide consoles us a little, and frightens us a lot.

You never realize how tacky your furniture is till you try to give some to the Salvation Army, and they won't take it.

When you let money speak for you, it drowns out anything else you meant to say.

A high salary is the slender thread that many a neurotic ego hangs by.

Money is much more exciting than anything it buys.

There are a handful of people whom money won't spoil, and we all count ourselves among them.

There's nothing quite so maddening to a woman as to be prepared to spend too much for a new dress, and then not be able to find one.

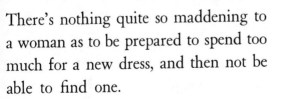
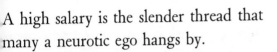
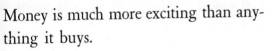

People who throw their money away aren't after money.

If you have money, just *assume* that people are after it, and go on from there.

Be glad that you're greedy; the national economy would collapse if you weren't.

Advice to shopkeepers, restaurant owners, *et al.*: Wildly overcharge; then when you lose a customer, it needn't wound your *amour propre*.

We're all born brave, trusting, and greedy, and most of us remain greedy.

Money is such a nice, clean, tellable, interesting thing to be worried about.

Even the most extravagant people have one thing they're terribly thrifty about—usually stamps.

I never throw good money after bad; my money has no morality.

I forget what it is that butters no parsnips, but I assume it's the high-priced spread.

We look forward to Christmas, forgetting from one year to the next how expensive and disappointing it was.

When you lose your money, you find out who your friends are—and they're not the ones you wanted.

Most people live within, or beyond, their income, to the same exact percentage, no matter how greatly the income itself varies.

Money is an expensive way to get rid of people, but cheapest in the long run.

When real pleasures fade, there's always the stock market.

Each day, the American housewife turns toward television as toward a lover. She feels guilty about it, and well she might, for he's covered with warts and is only after her money.

Instructions for the neurotic who can't afford an analyst: Ask yourself what advice he might give you; then follow the advice; then put the fee in the bank.

Money: in its absence, we are coarse; in its presence, we are vulgar.

I wish I'd said it first, and I don't even know who did: The only problems that money can solve are money problems.

Neurotics look on sex and money as just two more weapons.

Those without money often say they would do anything for it, when all they mean is that they would do anything pleasant and convenient. That's why only the rich are rich.

For the most selfish and happy life: spend all your money on yourself when you're young, then on your children as you grow older.

Artists refuse to accept the idea that they should starve; they want all the money, as well as all the fun.

The rich and the poor buy for cash; the middle class charges. And charges. And charges.

Too much money is as demoralizing as too little, and there's no such thing as exactly enough.

The habit of saving money is hard to
acquire, and even harder to break.

How to enter an expensive restaurant:
look as though you'd just bought it.

If you put your money where your
mouth is, you're going to have awfully
green teeth.

Anything you lose automatically dou-
bles in value.

If you charge it, all children and most
women will think it doesn't cost anything.

10 Years, Fears, and Other Follies

There are so many things that we wish we had done yesterday, so few that we feel like doing today.

A car is useless in New York, essential everywhere else. The same with good manners.

I've been observing, and have just come to a momentous conclusion: young love owes its life to the invention of tickling.

The two main hazards of psychoanalysis: that it might fail, and that if it succeeds, you'll never be able to forgive yourself for all those wasted years.

Today's music always sounds so cheesy to those who knew yesterday's.

In the bright lexicon of youth, there's no such word as "Yes."

Time-wasters a few decades ago were reading junky novels, which time-wasters today are watching old movies of, on television.

Luck: when your burst of energy doesn't run afoul of someone else's.

Vengefulness is self-pity's first cousin, loneliness its favorite climate, whisky its best friend.

The young quickly learn to love and be loved, to betray and be betrayed. The only further lesson maturity can teach them is how to keep from paying too high a price.

82

In choosing a mate, the young man relies largely on his sense of touch, the older man on his sense of humor.

We're charmed by coincidence, except when it inconveniences us.

When the terribly sincere voice on the TV commercial says "You see . . . ," you can take it to mean: Here comes the whopper.

The main difference between the tortured adolescent and the well-adjusted adult: the former's aghast to find that his mind is a cesspool; the latter accepts the fact that everyone's is.

Most neurotics die natural deaths, but they never thought they would.

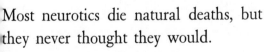

The young can seldom be faithless for long to the same person.

Spring, summer, and fall fill us with
hope; winter alone reminds us of the
human condition.

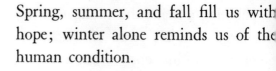

Flesh goes on pleasuring us, and hu-
miliating us, right to the end.

Indignation keeps many people alive,
and even keeps some of them
young.

Neurotics think of the past with resent-
ment, and the future with dread; the
present just doesn't exist.

When the salt has lost its savor, pepper
makes a poor substitute.

After twenty, we demand more of love,
but not with any practical hope of re-
ceiving it.

n months, not years, the mask becomes he face.

Healthy parakeets have the nervous energy of tennis players.

There's nothing that everybody would like to do, except maybe sing.

If there's one celebrity at the party, he'll spend the whole time with his clique; if there are two, they'll spend the whole time with each other.

Cigarettes are all the clock I need: one pack finishes the morning, another the afternoon, a third the night.

The sophisticate is always haughty when being introduced to a celebrity.

Your life is made up of years that mean nothing, moments that mean all.

There are people who get everything done, and people who get nothing done, and hardly anyone in between.

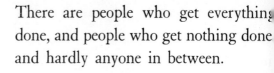

Don't you wish that TV commercials were twice as many fewer, and twice as much shorter?

There's nothing man has done that man cannot do better.

If you jot down every silly thought that pops into your head, you will soon find out everything you most seriously believe.

Aside to women who own jewelry: make a will, leaving each piece to a different young friend or relative. This is a very simple way of assuring yourself a little immortality. (Like Cyril Connolly, I define immortality as ten years.)

On the first day of spring there was a terrible snowstorm, and I felt I should atone for something.

The young couldn't care less about what people over thirty think.

The neurotic listens to weather reports about Small Craft Warnings, and he thinks: They're talking about me.

Loneliness, insomnia, and change: the fear of these is even worse than the reality.

There's no such thing as the Right Person, unless it's the Right Time.

For neurotics, success is a five-minute wonder; failure, a five-year plan.

It's innocence when it charms us, ignorance when it doesn't.

87

People have to be very old to die one at a time; young, they take a lot of others with them.

A face that's full of delight is *per se* a delightful face—except of course on television.

I know which side my bread is buttered on: the side which falls on the carpet.

Every human being is born wanting to do his best, at least until he tries it a few times and gets slapped down.

The women in a man's life do him credit, unless that's what he was counting on.

Regardless of the circumstances, a man never breaks off with a pretty woman who causes him absolutely no trouble.

A neurotic is someone who's afraid to see himself as he's afraid others see him.

I have an understanding with my husband: on any day when I haven't done any writing, I must play him three games of chess. The trouble is, if I *have* been working, I enjoy the chess; if not, all I want to play is Russian roulette.

Fine feathers make fine birds, until it comes time to fly.

I've started keeping files, so at last I'm methodical: I now know exactly how many months I let letters go unanswered.

Our strength is often composed of the weakness we're damned if we're going to show.

The human comedy can keep amusing you, but only if you keep your distance.

The neurotic's boat keeps drifting farther and farther out to sea, and people keep asking him why he's so nervous.

"Let's cut 'em off at the pass." This is frequently done to the villains in Westerns, and to the rest of us in real life.

If you let a situation get bad enough, every word you say will only make it worse.

It's the most unhappy people who most fear change.

A divorced person: one who, when angry, takes it out on whoever's nearest.

It's my hobby to collect teentsy celebrities. I find them on daytime television.

People determined to hide their feelings are usually nonstop talkers.

Why are people surprised when nice girls get into trouble? The ones who aren't nice know better.

Neurotics expect you to remember all the things that they tell you, and many that they don't.

Vanity, revenge, loneliness, boredom, all apply: lust is one of the least of the reasons for promiscuity.

Some hungry newspapers feed exclusively on scare headlines, and so do some hungry people.

Girls dread, more than any other blow of fate, a dateless Saturday night.

Whether or not *you* love television, you've got to admit that it certainly loves itself.

Recipe I've hit on, for a wonderful life: at least once a month, do something exciting that you've never done before. And please let me know how it comes out.

The young spend their time, *faute de mieux,* practicing on each other; but they don't want the old practicing on them too.

I'm glad I don't have to explain to a man from Mars why each day I set fire to dozens of little pieces of paper, and put them in my mouth.

If only we could be old and sick while we're still young and healthy enough to put up with it!

Sing it loud and clear: There's no vinism like *chau*vinism.

Each new non-prescription sleeping pill proudly advertises: "It's not habit-forming"—which naturally means go ahead and take it 365 nights a year.

Why I love my husband: he always bets on Hamilton Burger, and on the car without Platformate.

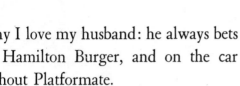

I love the idea of God tempering the wind to the shorn lamb, but I'd hate to have to sell it to an American Indian.

Epitaph for the human race: We've been terrible, but dear God how we've paid for it.

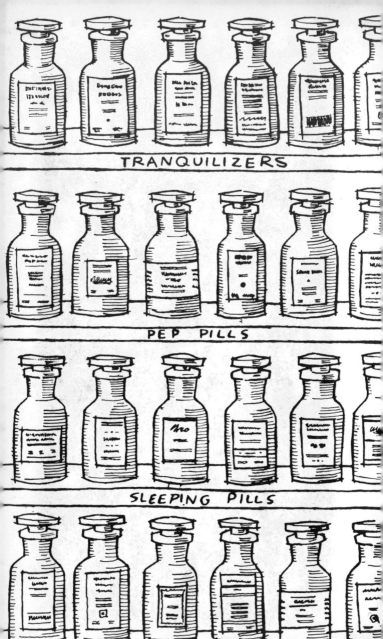

TRANQUILIZERS

PEP PILLS

SLEEPING PILLS

VITAMINS